Be Ye Inspired!
Volume III

Dr. C.

clfpublishing.org
909.315.3161

Copyright © 2024 by Cassundra White-Elliott.

All rights reserved. No portion of this book may be reproduced, stored in a retrieval system, or transmitted by any form or any means electronically, photocopied, recorded, or any other except for brief quotations in printed reviews, without the prior permission of the publisher.

Cover design by Senir Design. Contact info: info@senirdesign.com

ISBN #978-0-9857372-1-4
Printed in the United States of America.

Dedication

To all people, everywhere.

Acknowledgements

I acknowledge every trial, every circumstance, every person, every temptation, and every situation I encountered that led me to my knees, crying out to my Heavenly Father. I shed many tears as I sought the Lord's guidance. God is faithful and just. Each learning experience was an opportunity to add another ounce of substance to the woman I am today. Oh, bless His name!

Introduction

The purpose of **Be Ye Inspired!** is to provide an opportunity for a daily encounter with God. There are exactly 30 days of scripture and exhortation, one to be read each day of an average month. Make a point to read one per day; then, reflect on it. Allow the Holy Spirit to minister to you. You might even want to engage one of your friends in a daily discussion about the day's reading.

Cover image - The cover image was chosen because of the exuberant colors it contains and the beauty displayed within each flower petal. Each person is designed as intricately as a precious flower and goes through a unique process of growth and development where life has brought the person where he/she is today. Like a flower, you do not have much time to live. So, make the most of each day, and make your life count.

Day One

"Thou shalt not bow down to their gods, nor serve them, nor do after their works: but thou shalt utterly overthrow them, and quite break down their images. And ye shall serve the LORD your God, and he shall bless thy bread, and thy water; and I will take sickness away from the midst of thee. There shall nothing cast their young, nor be barren, in thy land: the number of thy days I will fulfil."

Exodus 23:24-26 (KJV)

"Do not bow down before their gods or worship them or follow their practices. You must demolish them and break their sacred stones to pieces. Worship the LORD your God, and his blessing will be on your food and water. I will take away sickness from among you, and none will miscarry or be barren in your land. I will give you a full life span."

Exodus 23:24-26 (NIV)

Practical Application

Exodus 23:24-26 provides a set of directives and promises that were originally given to the Israelites as they were preparing to enter the Promised Land.

Today's believers are encouraged to evaluate their lives and identify any 'idols' that might be taking precedence over their relationship with God. This could include excessive pursuit of wealth, status, or even technology. Their focus must be on maintaining a primary allegiance to God and His principles.

This translates into a wholehearted commitment to living out their faith. Serving God in every aspect of life - work, family, community - brings a complete sense of purpose and fulfillment. It's a reminder that true service to God encompasses all areas of life and not just religious observance, such as daily prayer and Sunday worship.

Believers today can take comfort in the assurance of God's provision and care. While physical health and prosperity are not guaranteed, the passage reinforces the idea that God is aware of our needs and is faithful in providing for them. Trusting in God's provision allows believers to focus on their spiritual health and growth.

This can be seen as a promise of fruitfulness and purpose in life. This does not only refer to physical offspring but can also be understood as being fruitful in one's endeavors and living a life of meaning and impact. Believers are encouraged to trust that God has a plan for their lives and that they can find fulfillment and purpose in following Him. These principles can guide believers in living lives that are devoted, purpose-driven, and reflective of God's love and faithfulness.

Day Two

"Though I speak with the tongues of men and of angels, and have not charity, I am become as sounding brass, or a tinkling cymbal. And though I have the gift of prophecy, and understand all mysteries, and all knowledge; and though I have all faith, so that I could remove mountains, and have not charity, I am nothing. And though I bestow all my goods to feed the poor, and though I give my body to be burned, and have not charity, it profiteth me nothing."

I Corinthians 13:1-3 (KJV)

"If I speak in the tongues of men or of angels, but do not have love, I am only a resounding gong or a clanging cymbal. If I have the gift of prophecy and can fathom all mysteries and all knowledge, and if I have a faith that can move mountains, but do not have love, I am nothing. If I give all I possess to the poor and give over my body to hardship that I may boast, but do not have love, I gain nothing."

I Corinthians 13:1-3 (NIV)

Practical Application

In our daily interactions, whether at work, home, or in social settings, effective communication is vital. This passage reminds us that no matter how eloquently we speak or how many languages we know, without love (charity), our words are empty. This means we should strive to communicate with kindness, patience, and sympathy. Listening actively and speaking gently can transform relationships and foster understanding.

It's easy to take pride in our talents, knowledge, or faith. However, Apostle Paul reminds us these gifts are meaningless without love. This calls us to approach our achievements and capabilities with humility, using them to serve and uplift others rather than seeking personal glory. Even our most generous acts, such as donating to charity or performing self-sacrificial deeds, must be motivated by love to have true value. In personal relationships, love should be the foundation. This means being patient, forgiving, and supportive even when it is difficult.

Love is not just about external actions but also about our internal state. Striving for inner peace and contentment and letting love guide our thoughts and actions can lead to a more fulfilling life.

Day Three

"As for me, I will call upon God; and the LORD shall save me. Evening, and morning, and at noon, will I pray, and cry aloud: and he shall hear my voice. He hath delivered my soul in peace from the battle that was against me: for there were many with me. Cast thy burden upon the LORD, and he shall sustain thee: he shall never suffer the righteous to be moved."

Psalm 55:16-18, 22 (KJV)

"But I call to God, and the LORD will save me. Evening and morning and at noon I utter my complaint and moan, and he hears my voice. He redeems my soul in safety from the battle that I wage, for many are arrayed against me. Cast your burden on the LORD, and he will sustain you; he will never permit the righteous to be moved."

Psalm 55:16-18, 22 (ESV)

Practical Application

Psalm 55:16-18 and 22 provide profound practical application for contemporary life, emphasizing reliance on God in times of distress and the power of consistent prayer. In today's world, filled with constant stressors and challenges, these verses encourage us to seek comfort in God, trusting that He listens and responds to our cries for help.

"But I call to God, and the Lord will save me." This reassures us that in moments of desperation, turning to God brings salvation. It teaches us to have faith that God's intervention is a source of deliverance.

"Evening and morning and at noon I utter my complaint and moan, and he hears my voice." This highlights the importance of regular, persistent prayer. Setting aside time throughout the day to connect with God can provide peace and clarity, helping us navigate daily struggles with a sense of divine support.

"He redeems my soul in safety from the battle that I wage, for many are arrayed against me." This verse reminds us that God offers protection and redemption even when we face overwhelming opposition. It encourages us to trust in God's omnipresence amidst life's battles.

"Cast your burden on the Lord, and he will sustain you; he will never permit the righteous to be moved." This is a call to release our anxieties to God, trusting Him to uphold and sustain us. It means letting go of worries, knowing God provides stability and strength to those who seek Him. By applying these principles, we can find spiritual resilience and inner peace in today's turbulent world.

Day Four

"Blessed be the God and Father of our Lord Jesus Christ, which according to his abundant mercy hath begotten us again unto a lively hope by the resurrection of Jesus Christ from the dead, to an inheritance incorruptible, and undefiled, and that fadeth not away, reserved in heaven for you, Who are kept by the power of God through faith unto salvation ready to be revealed in the last time.

I Peter 1:3-5 (KJV)

"Praise be to the God and Father of our Lord Jesus Christ! In his great mercy he has given us new birth into a living hope through the resurrection of Jesus Christ from the dead, and into an inheritance that can never perish, spoil or fade. This inheritance is kept in heaven for you, who through faith are shielded by God's power until the coming of the salvation that is ready to be revealed in the last time."

I Peter 1:3-5 (NIV)

Practical Application

I Peter 1:3-5 provides a profound message of hope and assurance, emphasizing the living hope through Jesus Christ, the inheritance awaiting us, and God's protection.

"Blessed be the God and Father of our Lord Jesus Christ! According to his great mercy, he has caused us to be born again to a living hope through the resurrection of Jesus Christ from the dead." In today's world, filled with uncertainty and challenges, this verse reminds us to focus on the living hope we have through Christ's resurrection. This hope is not fleeting; it is a steady anchor amidst life's storms. This means finding strength and motivation in the fact that our future is secure in Christ, no matter what we face daily.

"To an inheritance that is imperishable, undefiled, and unfading, kept in heaven for you." This encourages us to shift our perspective from earthly possessions and temporary gains to the eternal inheritance promised by God. It means living with an eternal mindset, prioritizing spiritual growth, and investing in relationships and actions that have lasting significance.

"Who by God's power are being guarded through faith for a salvation ready to be revealed in the last time." This assures us of God's continuous protection and support. It means trusting in God's power to guard us, even when circumstances seem overwhelming. This can be applied by developing a routine of prayer, relying on God's strength, and staying rooted in faith, knowing He is guarding our salvation.

Day Five

"Seek ye the LORD while he may be found, call ye upon him while he is near: Let the wicked forsake his way, and the unrighteous man his thoughts: and let him return unto the LORD, and he will have mercy upon him; and to our God, for he will abundantly pardon."

Isaiah 55:6-7 (KJV)

"Seek the LORD while he may be found; call on him while he is near. Let the wicked forsake their ways and the unrighteous their thoughts. Let them turn to the Lord, and he will have mercy on them, and to our God, for he will freely pardon."

Isaiah 55:6-7 (NIV)

Practical Application

Isaiah 55:6-7 provide a powerful call to action. These verses urge us to actively seek a relationship with God, emphasizing the urgency of turning to Him. In today's fast-paced world, where distractions are plentiful and spiritual connections can easily wane, this call is particularly pertinent to a strong spiritual posture.

"Seek the Lord while he may be found; call upon him while he is near." This encourages us to prioritize our spiritual life, making time for prayer, meditation, and scripture study. It serves as a reminder that our relationship with God requires proactive effort and consistent attention.

"Let the wicked forsake his way, and the unrighteous man his thoughts." This verse challenges us to self-reflect and recognize areas in our lives that need change. It calls for a conscious effort to abandon harmful behaviors and negative thought patterns. This means making better choices, cultivating positive habits, and seeking forgiveness for past wrongs.

"Let him return to the Lord, that he may have compassion on him, and to our God, for he will abundantly pardon." This underscores the boundless mercy and forgiveness God offers. It reassures us that no matter how far we have strayed, returning to God brings compassion and pardon. This means embracing repentance and seeking God's grace, leading to spiritual renewal and a fresh start.

By applying these verses today, we are encouraged to seek God earnestly, strive for moral integrity, and embrace His forgiveness, fostering a deeper, more resilient faith in our daily lives.

Day Six

"Then came Peter to him, and said, Lord, how oft shall my brother sin against me, and I forgive him? till seven times? Jesus saith unto him, I say not unto thee, Until seven times: but, Until seventy times seven."

Matthew 18:21-22 (KJV)

"Then Peter came to Jesus and asked, "Lord, how many times shall I forgive my brother or sister who sins against me? Up to seven times?" Jesus answered, "I tell you, not seven times, but seventy-seven times."

Matthew 18:21-22 (NIV)

Practical Application

Matthew 18:21-22 emphasize the importance of limitless forgiveness in our daily lives. Practically, this means embracing a mindset of compassion and understanding, even when others wrong us repeatedly. Here's how we can apply this teaching:

1. *Cultivate a forgiving attitude*: Recognize that everyone makes mistakes. Instead of holding grudges, focus on letting go of resentment. This reduces personal stress and promotes healthier relationships.

2. *Practice empathy*: Try to understand the perspective and circumstances of those who hurt you. This can make it easier to forgive and fosters a deeper connection and understanding with others.

3. *Set boundaries with grace*: While forgiveness is essential, it doesn't mean tolerating harmful behavior. Set healthy boundaries to protect yourself, but do so with a forgiving heart, wishing the best for the other person.

4. *Reflect on personal shortcomings*: Remember times when you needed forgiveness. This humility can help you extend the same grace to others.

5. *Promote peace*: Forgiveness is a powerful tool for conflict resolution. By choosing to forgive, you contribute to a more peaceful and cooperative environment at home, work, and in your community.

By incorporating these practices into daily life, we honor Jesus' teachings and create a more compassionate and understanding world.

Day Seven

"Now the God of peace, that brought again from the dead our Lord Jesus, that great shepherd of the sheep, through the blood of the everlasting covenant, Make you perfect in every good work to do his will, working in you that which is wellpleasing in his sight, through Jesus Christ; to whom be glory for ever and ever. Amen."

Hebrews 13:20-21 (KJV)

"Now may the God of peace, who through the blood of the eternal covenant brought back from the dead our Lord Jesus, that great Shepherd of the sheep, equip you with everything good for doing his will, and may he work in us what is pleasing to him, through Jesus Christ, to whom be glory for ever and ever. Amen."

Hebrews 13:20-21 (NIV)

Practical Application

Verse 20 begins by referring to God as the *"God of peace."* In a world filled with turmoil and anxiety, turning to God for peace can provide calm and stability. This means prioritizing moments of quiet reflection and prayer, seeking God's peace amidst daily chaos.

Recognizing Jesus as the *"great Shepherd of the sheep"* encourages us to follow His guidance and leadership. This involves studying His teachings and striving to emulate His love, compassion, and humility in our interactions with others.

The prayer that God *"equip you with everything good for doing his will"* highlights the importance of seeking God's provision in our endeavors. This means actively seeking to develop our talents and abilities, trusting that God will provide what we need to fulfill His purposes.

The desire for God to *"work in us what is pleasing to him"* calls us to align our actions with God's will. This involves making ethical decisions, showing kindness, and acting with integrity in our daily lives.

Finally, acknowledging that all glory belongs to Jesus reminds us to remain humble and give credit to God for our successes. This encourages a spirit of gratitude and recognition of God's role in our achievements.

By applying these principles, we can live a life that reflects our faith, bringing peace, purpose, and praise to God in our daily actions.

Day Eight

"The fear of the LORD prolongeth days: but the years of the wicked shall be shortened. The hope of the righteous shall be gladness: but the expectation of the wicked shall perish. The way of the LORD is strength to the upright: but destruction shall be to the workers of iniquity. The righteous shall never be removed: but the wicked shall not inhabit the earth. The mouth of the just bringeth forth wisdom: but the froward tongue shall be cut out. The lips of the righteous know what is acceptable: but the mouth of the wicked speaketh frowardness."

Proverbs 10:27-32 (KJV)

"The fear of the LORD prolongs life, but the years of the wicked will be short. The hope of the righteous brings joy, but the expectation of the wicked will perish. The way of the LORD is a stronghold to the blameless, but destruction to evildoers. The righteous will never be removed, but the wicked will not dwell in the land. The mouth of the righteous brings forth wisdom, but the perverse tongue will be cut off. The lips of the righteous know what is acceptable, but the mouth of the wicked, what is perverse."

Proverbs 10:27-32 (ESV)

Practical Application

Proverbs 10:27-32 focus on the benefits of living a righteous life and the consequences of wickedness. *"The fear of the Lord prolongs life, but the years of the wicked will be short."* This verse demonstrates the importance of living a life guided by reverence for God by leading an ethical and morally upright life.

"The hope of the righteous brings joy, but the expectation of the wicked will perish." This verse encourages us to foster hope and resilience, knowing that living righteously leads to lasting contentment, whereas deceit and malice lead to disappointment.

"The way of the Lord is a stronghold to the blameless, but destruction to evildoers." This reinforces that aligning with God's principles provides a foundation of security. *"The righteous will never be removed, but the wicked will not dwell in the land."* This speaks to the enduring legacy of righteous living versus the transient nature of wickedness. It encourages building a life of lasting value and positive impact, rather than seeking short-term gains through unethical means.

"The mouth of the righteous brings forth wisdom, but the perverse tongue will be cut off." This advises speaking truthfully and wisely. It promotes clear, honest communication and warns against the harm caused by deceit and manipulation. *"The lips of the righteous know what is acceptable, but the mouth of the wicked, what is perverse."* This verse teaches discernment in speech, advocating for respectful and constructive dialogue over harmful and destructive communication.

Day Nine

"For the wrath of God is revealed from heaven against all ungodliness and unrighteousness of men, who hold the truth in unrighteousness; Because that which may be known of God is manifest in them; for God hath shewed it unto them. For the invisible things of him from the creation of the world are clearly seen, being understood by the things that are made, even his eternal power and Godhead; so that they are without excuse."

Romans 1:18-20 (KJV)

"The wrath of God is being revealed from heaven against all the godlessness and wickedness of people, who suppress the truth by their wickedness, since what may be known about God is plain to them, because God has made it plain to them. For since the creation of the world God's invisible qualities—his eternal power and divine nature—have been clearly seen, being understood from what has been made, so that people are without excuse."

Romans 1:18-20 (NIV)

Practical Application

In today's world, these verses offer a powerful reminder about the reality and visibility of God's presence and moral expectations. They emphasize God's nature and power are evident in creation, making spiritual ignorance indefensible.

Here's how to apply these principles:

1. Take time to observe the natural world. Whether it's a walk in the park or appreciating a sunset, let the beauty and complexity of creation remind you of God's power and divinity.

2. Reflect on personal behavior and align it with God's standards. Avoid actions that suppress truth and promote unrighteousness. Strive to live a life that reflects godliness.

3. Be proactive in seeking and acknowledging the truth about God. This can involve studying scripture, engaging in discussions about faith, and being open to the evidence of God's presence in everyday life.

4. Share these truths with others, encouraging them to recognize God in their lives and live righteously. This can foster a community grounded in mutual respect and spiritual awareness.

Day Ten

"This book of the law shall not depart out of thy mouth; but thou shalt meditate therein day and night, that thou mayest observe to do according to all that is written therein: for then thou shalt make thy way prosperous, and then thou shalt have good success. Have not I commanded thee? Be strong and of a good courage; be not afraid, neither be thou dismayed: for the LORD thy God is with thee whithersoever thou goest."

Joshua1:8-9 (KJV)

"Keep this Book of the Law always on your lips; meditate on it day and night, so that you may be careful to do everything written in it. Then you will be prosperous and successful. Have I not commanded you? Be strong and courageous. Do not be afraid; do not be discouraged, for the LORD your God will be with you wherever you go."

Joshua1:8-9 (NIV)

Practical Application

The command to meditate on the Book of the Law day and night emphasizes the importance of regularly engaging with the Bible. This means setting aside time each day for reading, studying, and reflecting on Scripture. This practice can guide our actions, influence our decisions, and align our lives with God's will.

The verses encourage us not only to read but to act according to what is written. Applying biblical principles in our daily interactions and choices leads to a life marked by integrity and purpose. This practical obedience brings about true prosperity and success as defined by God's standards.

God's command to be strong and courageous is a call to face life's challenges with confidence, knowing we are not alone. This means trusting God in uncertain times, standing firm in our faith despite difficulties, and moving forward with the assurance of His presence.

The reminder not to be frightened or dismayed addresses the common human experiences of fear and anxiety. By leaning on God's promises and His constant presence, we can find peace and strength to navigate stressful situations.

Day Eleven

*"I cried unto him with my mouth,
and he was extolled with my tongue.
If I regard iniquity in my heart,
the Lord will not hear me:
But verily God hath heard me;
he hath attended to the voice
of my prayer. Blessed be God,
which hath not turned away my
prayer, nor his mercy from me."*

Psalm 66:17-20 (KJV)

*"I cried out to him with my mouth;
his praise was on my tongue.
If I had cherished sin in my heart,
the Lord would not have listened;
but God has surely listened
and has heard my prayer.
Praise be to God,
who has not rejected my prayer
or withheld his love from me!"*

Psalm 66:17-20 (NIV)

Practical Application

"I cried out to him with my mouth; his praise was on my tongue." This reminds us to be open and honest with God in our prayers. Expressing our true feelings and needs, while also praising Him, fosters a sincere connection. During life's daily happenings, setting aside dedicated time for such heartfelt communication can provide clarity and comfort.

"If I had cherished sin in my heart, the Lord would not have listened." This verse highlights the necessity of repentance and striving for purity. Acknowledging and turning away from our wrongdoings allows us to maintain a clear conscience and a stronger spiritual connection. Regular self-reflection and seeking forgiveness help keep our hearts aligned with God's will.

"But God has surely listened and has heard my prayer." This assures us of God's attentiveness and responsiveness. Trusting that God hears and cares for us can bring immense peace, especially during challenging times. It encourages persistence in prayer, knowing God is always listening.

"Praise be to God, who has not rejected my prayer or withheld his love from me!" This calls us to continually thank and praise God for His unwavering love and faithfulness. Cultivating an attitude of gratitude, even in difficult circumstances, can transform our perspective and enhance our overall well-being.

Day Twelve

"Now the God of peace, that brought again from the dead our Lord Jesus, that great shepherd of the sheep, through the blood of the everlasting covenant, Make you perfect in every good work to do his will, working in you that which is wellpleasing in his sight, through Jesus Christ; to whom be glory for ever and ever." Amen."

Hebrews 13:20-21 (KJV)

"Now may the God of peace, who through the blood of the eternal covenant brought back from the dead our Lord Jesus, that great Shepherd of the sheep, equip you with everything good for doing his will, and may he work in us what is pleasing to him, through Jesus Christ, to whom be glory for ever and ever. Amen."

Hebrews 13:20-21 (NIV)

Practical Application

These verses highlight God's role as a peace-giver and provider, emphasizing the resurrection of Jesus and the eternal covenant as the foundation of our faith. Here's how the verses can be applied today:

In a world filled with turmoil and conflict, this verse reminds us that true peace comes from God. We can turn to Him for calmness and reassurance in our daily lives, trusting in His divine peace to guide us through challenging times.

Understanding Jesus as the *"great Shepherd"* underscores His role in guiding and protecting us. We can lean on His wisdom and direction, knowing He leads us with care and love.

The prayer that God equips us with *"everything good for doing his will"* encourages us to actively seek and utilize the talents and resources God provides. This means engaging in acts of kindness, serving others, and fulfilling our unique callings with the abilities God has given us.

Allowing God to *"work in us what is pleasing to him"* suggests a continuous, humble submission to His will. We can make a daily practice of seeking His guidance in our decisions, aiming to live in ways that honor and please Him.

Finally, recognizing that all glory belongs to Jesus prompts us to live in a manner that reflects His love and grace. This involves sharing our faith, acting with integrity, and giving thanks for His everlasting covenant.

Day Thirteen

"Then Job arose, and rent his mantle, and shaved his head, and fell down upon the ground, and worshipped, And said, Naked came I out of my mother's womb, and naked shall I return thither: the Lord gave, and the Lord hath taken away; blessed be the name of the Lord. In all t his Job sinned not, nor charged God foolishly."

Job 1:20-22 (KJV)

"Then Job arose and tore his robe and shaved his head and fell on the ground and worshiped. And he said, 'Naked I came from my mother's womb, and naked shall I return. The L<small>ORD</small> gave, and the L<small>ORD</small> has taken away; blessed be the name of the L<small>ORD</small>.' In all this Job did not sin or charge God with wrong."

Job 1:20-22 (ESV)

Practical Application

When confronted with personal tragedy or hardship, it's natural to feel deep sorrow and grief. Job's actions - tearing his robe and shaving his head - demonstrated an honest expression of anguish. However, despite his intense suffering, Job still worshiped God. Today, this teaches us that it is possible to maintain our faith and turn to God even when we are in pain. Instead of becoming bitter or turning away from God, we can choose to seek His presence and find solace in worship.

Job acknowledged the temporary nature of earthly possessions and life itself. By recognizing that everything we have is a gift from God, we can cultivate a mindset of gratitude and humility. Today, this can help us cope with loss by understanding that our identity and worth are not tied to our material possessions or circumstances but are rooted in our relationship with God. Embracing this perspective can lead to inner peace and resilience.

Maintaining integrity and faith during trials is a testament to spiritual maturity. Job's refusal to blame God for his suffering encourages us to trust in God's goodness and sovereignty, even when we don't understand why we are facing difficulties. This trust can sustain us through challenging times, allowing us to grow stronger in our faith and character.

Day Fourteen

"Blessed is the man that trusteth in the LORD, and whose hope the LORD is. For he shall be as a tree planted by the waters, and that spreadeth out her roots by the river, and shall not see when heat cometh, but her leaf shall be green; and shall not be careful in the year of drought, neither shall cease from yielding fruit."

Jeremiah 17:7-8 (KJV)

"But blessed is the one who trusts in the Lord, whose confidence is in him. They will be like a tree planted by the water that sends out its roots by the stream. It does not fear when heat comes; its leaves are always green. It has no worries in a year of drought and never fails to bear fruit."

Jeremiah 17:7-8 (NIV)

Practical Application

In today's world, where uncertainty and challenges are rampant, these verses encourage us to place our trust in God. Trusting in God means believing in His plan and wisdom, even when circumstances are difficult or unclear. This trust is not passive; rather, it involves actively seeking God's guidance through prayer, meditation, and reading His Word.

The imagery of a tree planted by the water signifies stability and nourishment. By placing our confidence in God, we root ourselves in a source of strength that sustains us through life's trials. Like the tree that remains green and fruitful even in adverse conditions, those who trust in God can find peace and productivity regardless of external circumstances.

Collectively, this means cultivating a daily habit of relying on God. It involves surrendering our worries and fears to Him, trusting that He will provide and sustain us. This trust leads to a life marked by inner peace and the ability to thrive and bear fruit, even in challenging times. By deeply rooting our lives in faith, we become resilient and unwavering, reflecting the steadfastness described in these verses.

Day Fifteen

"Grace and peace be multiplied unto you through the knowledge of God, and of Jesus our Lord, According as his divine power hath given unto us all things that pertain unto life and godliness, through the knowledge of him that hath called us to glory and virtue: Whereby are given unto us exceeding great and precious promises: that by these ye might be partakers of the divine nature, having escaped the corruption that is in the world through lust."

II Peter 1:2-4 (KJV)

"Grace and peace be yours in abundance through the knowledge of God and of Jesus our Lord. His divine power has given us everything we need for a godly life through our knowledge of him who called us by his own glory and goodness. Through these he has given us his very great and precious promises, so that through them you may participate in the divine nature, having escaped the corruption in the world caused by evil desires."

II Peter 1:2-4 (NIV)

Practical Application

These verses from II Peter remind us that through our relationship with God and Jesus, we are endowed with grace, peace, and the divine power necessary for living a godly life. In today's context, this means actively seeking to know God and Jesus more intimately through prayer, study of scripture, and worship, which in turn ushers in an abundance of grace and peace into our lives.

We are assured that everything we need for a life of righteousness has already been provided to us. This encourages us to trust in God's provision and guidance, especially when facing moral and ethical challenges. By embracing God's promises, we can overcome temptations and the corruption prevalent in the world, striving to live with integrity and purpose.

Furthermore, recognizing we are called and chosen by God, His goodness motivates us to reflect these attributes in our daily interactions. This includes showing kindness, practicing patience, and standing up for justice. Ultimately, these verses challenge us to participate in God's divine nature by embodying Christ-like qualities, thus transforming not only our lives but also the lives of those around us.

Day Sixteen

"But ye shall receive power, after that the Holy Ghost is come upon you: and ye shall be witnesses unto me both in Jerusalem, and in all Judaea, and in Samaria, and unto the uttermost part of the earth."

Acts 1-8 (KJV)

"But you will receive power when the Holy Spirit comes on you; and you will be my witnesses in Jerusalem, and in all Judea and Samaria, and to the ends of the earth."

Acts 1:8 (NIV)

Practical Application

Acts 1:8 emphasizes the empowerment of believers through the infilling of Holy Spirit to be witnesses of Christ's message. Today, this can be practically applied in several ways. First, believers are encouraged to seek a personal relationship with Holy Spirit through prayer and study of the Scriptures, allowing His power to guide and strengthen them.

Second, being witnesses "in Jerusalem, and in all Judea and Samaria, and to the ends of the earth" translates to sharing the message of love, hope, and redemption starting from one's immediate community (family, friends, and local community) and extending to broader spheres (workplace, social networks, and even globally). This can be done through acts of kindness, participating in community service, and using various platforms, including social media, to share personal testimonies and encouraging messages.

Moreover, this verse calls for cultural sensitivity and inclusivity, as believers are to reach out beyond their comfort zones and embrace people from diverse backgrounds, promoting unity and understanding. It encourages stepping out in faith, trusting that Holy Spirit will provide the necessary boldness and wisdom to effectively communicate and live out the teachings of Jesus in everyday life.

By embodying the principles of love, service, and witness as outlined in Acts 1:8, believers can make a meaningful impact in their communities and beyond, reflecting Holy Spirit's transformative power in a contemporary world.

Day Seventeen

"The Lord shall preserve thee from all evil: he shall preserve thy soul. The Lord shall preserve thy going out and thy coming in from this time forth, and even for evermore."

Psalm 121:7-8 (KJV)

"The LORD will keep you from all harm - he will watch over your life; the LORD will watch over your coming and going both now and forevermore."

Psalm 121:7-8 (NIV)

Practical Application

This passage offers profound comfort and assurance in our daily lives. It reminds us that God's protection is not limited to specific moments but extends throughout our entire journey. Whether we are embarking on a new challenge, facing difficult decisions, or simply going about our everyday routines, we can trust that God is vigilantly watching over us.

These verses encourage us to live with confidence, knowing we are never alone. They can be applied by consciously placing our trust in God's care in every situation, big or small. When anxiety or fear arises, we can reflect on these verses to reinforce our faith that God is actively guarding our paths and keeping a hedge of protection around us.

Moreover, this passage invites us to start and end our days with prayer, asking for God's guidance and protection. By doing so, we align ourselves with the assurance that God's watchful presence surrounds us, bringing peace to our hearts and minds as we navigate the complexities of life.

Day Eighteen

"The eyes of your understanding being enlightened; that ye may know what is the hope of his calling, and what the riches of the glory of his inheritance in the saints. And what is the exceeding greatness of his power to us-ward who believe, according to the working of his mighty power, Which he wrought in Christ, when he raised him from the dead, and set him at his own right hand in the heavenly places, Far above all principality, and power, and might, and dominion, and every name that is named, not only in this world, but also in that which is to come:"
Ephesians 1:18-21 (KJV)

"I pray that the eyes of your heart may be enlightened, so that you will know what is the hope of His calling, what are the riches of the glory of His inheritance in the saints, and what is the boundless greatness of His power toward us who believe. These are in accordance with the working of the strength of His might which He brought about in Christ, when He raised Him from the dead and seated Him at His right hand in the heavenly places, far above all rule and authority and power and dominion, and every name that is named, not only in this age but also in the one to come."
Ephesians 1:18-21 (NASB)

Practical Application

Ephesians 1:18-21 calls us to understand the incredible power and hope we have as believers in Christ. Practically applying this passage involves recognizing the riches of God's grace in our daily lives and living with a deep sense of purpose and confidence.

First, we should pray for spiritual enlightenment, asking God to open the eyes of our hearts to see the hope we have in Him. This helps us live with a perspective rooted in eternity, rather than being consumed by the temporary challenges of life.

Second, we can draw strength from knowing the same power that raised Christ from the dead is at work within us. This empowers us to face difficulties with faith, knowing God's power can bring transformation and victory in any situation.

Finally, understanding our identity as God's inheritance reminds us that we are deeply valued by Him. This should inspire us to live in a way that reflects our worth and calling, engaging in actions that honor God and serve others.

By embracing these truths, we can live with greater hope, resilience, and purpose, knowing God's mighty power is always available to us.

Day Nineteen

"And when ye stand praying, forgive, if ye have ought against any: that your Father also which is in heaven may forgive you your trespasses."

Mark 11:25 (KJV)

"And whenever you stand praying, forgive, if you have anything against anyone, so that your Father also who is in heaven may forgive you your trespasses."

Mark 11:25 (ESV)

Practical Application

This verse emphasizes the importance of forgiveness in our daily lives. When we hold onto grudges or harbor resentment, it creates a barrier between us and God, affecting our spiritual well-being. Forgiveness is not just a suggestion; it is a command that directly impacts our relationship with God and others.

In practice, this means actively choosing to let go of anger and bitterness, even when it's difficult. Before we pray or seek God's guidance, we should examine our hearts and forgive those who have wronged us. This act of forgiveness releases us from the burden of negative emotions, fosters inner peace, and aligns us with God's will.

Forgiving others doesn't mean excusing their behavior, but it does mean releasing the hold that the hurt has on our hearts. By practicing forgiveness, we open ourselves to receive God's forgiveness and maintain a healthy, loving relationship with Him and those around us. This daily application transforms our hearts, promotes healing, and reflects the grace we've received from God.

Day Twenty

"The LORD is my strength and my shield; my heart trusted in him, and I am helped: therefore my heart greatly rejoiceth; and with my song will I praise him."

Psalm 28:7 (KJV)

"The Lord is my strength and my shield; my heart trusts in him, and he helps me. My heart leaps for joy, and with my song I praise him."

Psalm 28:7 (NIV)

Practical Application

This verse serves as a powerful reminder that in times of challenge or uncertainty, we can rely on God as our source of strength and protection. Practically, this means turning to God in prayer and trusting in His provision when we feel overwhelmed or fearful. Instead of relying solely on our own abilities, we acknowledge our dependence on God, who empowers us to face difficulties with courage and resilience.

When we trust in God, we experience a peace that allows us to remain joyful even in tough situations. This joy becomes a testimony of God's faithfulness, prompting us to praise Him openly. We can live out this verse by expressing gratitude daily, not only when things go well but also when we face adversity. Singing songs of praise or simply speaking words of thankfulness shifts our focus from our problems to God's goodness, reinforcing our trust in Him and strengthening our faith.

Applying Psalm 28:7 in our lives fosters a mindset of trust, gratitude, and praise, helping us navigate life's challenges with confidence in God's unwavering support.

Day Twenty-One

"Then said Jesus to those Jews which believed on him, If ye continue in my word, then are ye my disciples indeed; And ye shall know the truth, and the truth shall make you free."

John 8:31-32 (KJV)

"To the Jews who had believed him, Jesus said, "If you hold to my teaching, you are really my disciples. Then you will know the truth, and the truth will set you free."

John 8:31-32 (NIV)

Practical Application

Practically applying this verse involves living in alignment with Jesus' teachings, which are rooted in love, forgiveness, and integrity. By consistently practicing these values in our daily lives - whether in relationships, work, or personal decisions - we embody true discipleship.

Understanding and embracing the truth of God's Word brings spiritual freedom, liberating us from the bondage of sin, guilt, and fear. This truth challenges us to confront and shed falsehoods, whether they are internal lies we tell ourselves or external deceptions from society. In a world where misinformation and moral decay are rampant, adhering to Jesus' teachings provides a clear, unwavering foundation. This leads to a life characterized by peace, purpose, and authenticity. By living out these principles, we not only experience personal transformation but also positively influence those around us, contributing to a more just and compassionate world.

Day Twenty-Two

"There is therefore now no condemnation to them which are in Christ Jesus, who walk not after the flesh, but after the Spirit. For the law of the Spirit of life in Christ Jesus hath made me free from the law of sin and death."

Romans 8:1-2 (KJV)

"Therefore, there is now no condemnation for those who are in Christ Jesus, because through Christ Jesus the law of the Spirit who gives life has set you free from the law of sin and death."

Romans 8:1-2 (NIV)

Practical Application

This passage means living with the assurance that, in Christ, you are no longer condemned by your past mistakes or sins. This freedom allows you to let go of guilt and shame, knowing Christ's sacrifice has paid the penalty for your sins. It encourages you to live a life led by the Spirit, focusing on the transformative power of God's grace rather than being trapped in legalism or self-condemnation, as those who attempt to live according to the law rather than under God's grace..

In everyday life, this means embracing forgiveness - both receiving it and extending it to others. It encourages you to reject fear and anxiety about your spiritual standing, replacing it with confidence in God's love and grace. This passage also calls you to walk in newness of life, making choices that reflect your identity in Christ, empowered by the Holy Spirit to overcome sinful habits and live in freedom. Ultimately, it's about living a life rooted in the assurance of God's love and grace, leading to inner peace and spiritual growth.

Day Twenty-Three

"Are not five sparrows sold for two farthings, and not one of them is forgotten before God? But even the very hairs of your head are all numbered. Fear not therefore: ye are of more value than many sparrows."

Luke 12:6-7 (KJV)

"What is the price of five sparrows – two copper coins? Yet God does not forget a single one of them. And the very hairs on your head are all numbered. So don't be afraid; you are more valuable to God than a whole flock of sparrows."

Luke 12:6-7 (NLT)

Practical Application

Luke 12:6-7 teaches that God values and cares deeply for each of us, even knowing the number of hairs on our heads. In daily life, this scripture encourages us to live with confidence and peace, knowing we are valued and cherished by God.

Practically, this can be applied by embracing a mindset of trust rather than worry. When facing challenges, remind yourself if God cares for the sparrows, He certainly cares for you, so there's no need to be consumed by anxiety about the future. This perspective can lead to a more grounded and serene approach to life, where you make decisions with the assurance you are under God's watchful care.

Additionally, this passage calls us to recognize our inherent worth and to treat others with the same dignity and respect, knowing they too are deeply valued by God. In interactions with others, practicing kindness, patience, and understanding becomes a reflection of the care God shows towards all His creations. By living in this way, we align our daily actions with the profound truth of God's attentive love.

Day Twenty-Four

"And therefore will the LORD wait, that he may be gracious unto you, and therefore will he be exalted, that he may have mercy upon you: for the LORD is a God of judgment: blessed are all they that wait for him."

Isaiah 30:18 (KJV)

"Yet the Lord longs to be gracious to you; therefore he will rise up to show you compassion. For the Lord is a God of justice. Blessed are all who wait for him!"

Isaiah 30:18 (NIV)

Practical Application

Isaiah 30:18 emphasizes God's patience and desire to show grace and compassion to those who wait on Him. To apply this verse daily, start by cultivating patience in your life. Trust in God's timing rather than forcing your own plans. When faced with challenges or delays, remember God is working behind the scenes for your good.

Begin your day with prayer, asking for the strength to remain patient and to recognize God's hand in all situations. Throughout the day, practice mindfulness, pausing to reflect on how God's grace has been evident in your life. Be compassionate towards others, as God is towards you - extend grace, forgiveness, and understanding even when it's difficult.

When things don't go as planned, remind yourself that waiting on God isn't passive; it's an active trust in His wisdom and love. Look for opportunities to serve others, knowing God uses these moments to build character and faith. End your day with gratitude, acknowledging how God's timing, though sometimes mysterious, has always been perfect. This daily practice not only deepens your faith but also aligns your life with God's compassionate and gracious nature.

Day Twenty-Five

"For the word of God is quick, and powerful, and sharper than any twoedged sword, piercing even to the dividing asunder of soul and spirit, and of the joints and marrow, and is a discerner of the thoughts and intents of the heart."

Hebrews 4:12 (KJV)

"For the word of God is alive and active. Sharper than any double-edged sword, it penetrates even to dividing soul and spirit, joints and marrow; it judges the thoughts and attitudes of the heart."

Hebrews 4:12 (NIV)

Practical Application

Hebrews 4:12 emphasizes the power and precision of God's Word, describing it as "living and active, sharper than any double-edged sword." This verse serves as a daily reminder of the importance of engaging with Scripture to navigate life's challenges. Practically applying this involves starting each day focusing on the Bible, allowing its teachings to shape your thoughts, actions, and decisions.

When faced with difficult situations or moral dilemmas, reflecting on biblical principles helps in discerning right from wrong. For instance, the verse encourages self-examination, challenging believers to align their inner motives and outward behaviors with God's will. It acts as a guide, cutting through confusion and providing clarity and conviction.

Additionally, Hebrews 4:12 serves as a tool for personal growth, encouraging the shedding of unhealthy habits or thoughts that do not align with a Christ-centered life. By consistently returning to Scripture, believers can cultivate a deeper relationship with God, ensuring their lives reflect His truth and grace. Ultimately, this daily engagement with God's Word equips individuals to live purposefully, with integrity and spiritual insight.

Day Twenty-Six

"For if there be first a willing mind, it is accepted according to that a man hath, and not according to that he hath not. For I mean not that other men be eased, and ye burdened: But by an equality, that now at this time your abundance may be a supply for their want, that their abundance also may be a supply for your want: that there may be equality."

II Corinthians 8:12-14 (KJV)

"For if the readiness is there, it is acceptable according as a man hath, not according as he hath not. For I say not this that others may be eased and ye distressed; but by equality: your abundance being a supply at this present time for their want, that their abundance also may become a supply for your want; that there may be equality."

II Corinthians 8:12-14 (ASV)

Practical Application

II Corinthians 8:12-14 emphasizes the importance of giving with a willing heart, not based on the amount, but on one's willingness and ability to give. It teaches us that the readiness to help others is what matters most, and that generosity should be practiced according to what one has, not what one lacks. This passage encourages a balance, where those who have more can do more to assist those in need, creating a sense of equality.

In daily life, this can be applied by being mindful of the needs of others and giving from a place of genuine desire to help, rather than obligation or comparison. Whether it's offering time, resources, or emotional support, the key is to give what we can without overextending ourselves. For example, sharing a meal with someone who might be struggling or offering a listening ear to a friend in distress are ways to embody this teaching. By focusing on the act of giving, rather than the amount, we contribute to a community where everyone's needs are met, fostering mutual care and support. This daily practice not only helps others but also cultivates a spirit of gratitude to the Father for the provisions He has made for us as well as contentment within ourselves.

Day Twenty-Seven

"Be it known unto you therefore, men and brethren, that through this man is preached unto you the forgiveness of sins: And by him all that believe are justified from all things, from which ye could not be justified by the law of Moses."

Acts 13:38-39 (KJV)

"Therefore, my friends, I want you to know that through Jesus the forgiveness of sins is proclaimed to you. Through him everyone who believes is set free from every sin, a justification you were not able to obtain under the law of Moses."

Acts 13:38-39 (NIV)

Practical Application

Acts 13:38-39 emphasize the forgiveness of sins through Jesus Christ, highlighting the liberation from the law that couldn't justify anyone. In daily life, this scripture reminds us of the grace we receive through faith, which is not earned by our deeds but given freely by God.

Practically, this means living with a deep sense of gratitude and humility, knowing our mistakes don't define us. It encourages us to forgive others as we have been forgiven, letting go of grudges and embracing reconciliation. By accepting God's grace, we are empowered to extend grace to others, fostering an environment of love and understanding.

Moreover, these verses call us to let go of legalism and self-reliance, trusting in God's mercy rather than our own ability to be "good enough." This frees us from the burden of perfectionism and allows us to live with joy and peace, confident in God's acceptance. Daily application involves a continuous turning to Christ, seeking His guidance and strength to live out our faith, and sharing the message of forgiveness with those around us. In this way, we embody the freedom and love that come from a relationship with Jesus.

Day Twenty-Eight

"Teach me thy way, O LORD, and lead me in a plain path, because of mine enemies. Deliver me not over unto the will of mine enemies: for false witnesses are risen up against me, and such as breathe out cruelty. I had fainted, unless I had believed to see the goodness of the LORD in the land of the living. Wait on the LORD: be of good courage, and he shall strengthen thine heart: wait, I say, on the LORD."

Psalm 27:11-14 (KJV)

"Teach me your way, O LORD, and lead me on a level path because of my enemies. Give me not up to the will of my adversaries; for false witnesses have risen against me, and they breathe out violence. I believe that I shall look upon the goodness of the LORD in the land of the living! Wait for the LORD; be strong, and let your heart take courage; wait for the LORD!"

Psalm 27:11-14 (ESV)

Practical Application

Psalm 27:11-14 encourages believers to seek God's guidance, trust in His protection, and remain patient in faith. Practically applying these verses daily involves starting your day by asking God for direction and wisdom in your decisions ("Teach me your way, O Lord"). This can be done through prayer and meditation on Scripture, seeking to align your actions with God's will.

As you go about your day, trust in God's protection even when faced with challenges or adversaries ("Do not deliver me to the will of my adversaries"). This trust can be manifested in maintaining peace and confidence, knowing God is your helper.

Patience is also key, especially when facing difficult situations or waiting for answers to prayers ("Wait for the Lord; be strong, and let your heart take courage"). Instead of rushing or acting out of fear, take time to breathe, pray, and wait on God's timing.

By consistently seeking God's guidance, trusting in His protection, and exercising patience, you can live out the principles of Psalm 27:11-14 in your daily life, growing in faith and resilience.

Day Twenty-Nine

"Now unto him that is able to do exceeding abundantly above all that we ask or think, according to the power that worketh in us, Unto him be glory in the church by Christ Jesus throughout all ages, world without end. Amen."

Ephesians 3:20-21 (KJV)

"Now to him who is able to do immeasurably more than all we ask or imagine, according to his power that is at work within us, to him be glory in the church and in Christ Jesus throughout all generations, for ever and ever! Amen."

Ephesians 3:20-21 (NIV)

Practical Application

Ephesians 3:20-21 reminds us that God is capable of doing far more than we can ask or imagine, according to His power at work within us. Practically applying this in daily life involves living with a mindset of faith and expectation. Each day, we can trust that God is at work in our circumstances, even when things seem challenging or uncertain.

Start your day by acknowledging God's greatness and surrendering your plans to Him, inviting His power to guide your actions and decisions. When faced with challenges, remind yourself that God's ability exceeds any problem, and seek His wisdom in your responses.

Practice gratitude, recognizing the small and large ways God exceeds your expectations. Share this hope with others, encouraging them to trust in God's power and faithfulness. Live with a spirit of generosity, knowing God can multiply your efforts far beyond what you can see.

Finally, give God glory in all things, understanding His work in and through your life is a testimony to His greatness. By doing so, you align yourself with His purposes and experience the fullness of life that He promises.

Day Thirty

"Be merciful unto me, O God: for man would swallow me up; he fighting daily oppresseth me. Mine enemies would daily swallow me up: for they be many that fight against me, O thou most High. What time I am afraid, I will trust in thee. In God I will praise his word, in God I have put my trust; I will not fear what flesh can do unto me."

Psalm 56:1-4 (KJV)

"Be merciful to me, my God, for my enemies are in hot pursuit; all day long they press their attack. My adversaries pursue me all day long; in their pride many are attacking me. When I am afraid, I put my trust in you. In God, whose word I praise – in God I trust and am not afraid. What can mere mortals do to me?"

Psalm 56:1-4 (NIV)

Practical Application

Psalm 56:1-4 speaks to seeking God's mercy and trusting Him in times of fear and adversity. Daily practical application of this passage involves cultivating a habit of turning to God when overwhelmed by challenges. When facing difficulties, instead of succumbing to anxiety, one can choose to pray, echoing the psalmist's confidence: *"When I am afraid, I put my trust in You."*

This trust is not passive but involves active reliance on God's promises. In daily life, this means consciously replacing fear with faith, recalling that God's Word is trustworthy. For example, when dealing with difficult situations at work, or personal conflicts, instead of letting fear dictate actions, pause and pray for guidance, believing God is in control.

Additionally, reflecting on God's past faithfulness can reinforce trust. Keeping a journal of answered prayers and moments of divine intervention can serve as a reminder that, as in the past, God is present and powerful today. In conversations, choose words that reflect faith rather than fear, encouraging others to trust God in their struggles as well. This practice fosters a lifestyle rooted in faith, where God's presence becomes the primary source of courage and peace.

Gift of Salvation for Non-Believers

"For all have sinned, and come short of the glory of God." (Romans 3:23)

This section was written especially for non-believers, those who have not accepted the gift of salvation. The gift of salvation saves souls from eternal damnation and is a free gift offered by God Himself.

John 3:16-18 says, *"For God so loved the world, that he gave his only begotten Son, that whosoever believeth in him should not perish, but have everlasting life. For God sent not his Son into the world to condemn the world; but that the world through him might be saved. He that believeth on him is not condemned: but he that believeth not is condemned already, because he hath not believed in the name of the only begotten Son of God."*

This section of scripture tells us God's purpose for giving His son Jesus to the world. The world was in a bad condition. The world was overwrought with sin; the people were living for fleshly desires rather than for God's desires.

As a result of the world's conditions, God decided He would offer the perfect sacrifice that would save the world from being a place where people were lost and had no hope. He decided His own son could stand in proxy for the sin-filled world, taking all sin upon Himself.

So Jesus came, born of a virgin, to save this dying world. He walked on this earth for 33 ½ years, doing the work of His Heavenly Father. At the appointed time, He died by way of crucifixion upon a cross at Calvary, on Golgotha's hill. He shed His blood and died for you and for me. Because His blood was pure, it paid the penalty for all unrighteousness and gave those who believe in Him direct access to His father's throne.

Scripture tells us in Matthew 27:51 that the veil of the temple was ripped in two from top to bottom, at the moment that Jesus' spirit left His body. As a result of the veil's removal, we are no longer required to have a high priest make intercession for us. We, as the children of the Most High God, are able to approach the throne of God for ourselves, and Jesus sits on the right hand of the Father making intercession for us.

But what is even more miraculous than God offering His own son as the perfect sacrifice was the fact that when Jesus was placed in grave clothes and placed in a tomb, He only remained there until the third day. God would not have it that His son would remain in the heart of the earth forever. In order for people to believe in the awesome power of God and His dear son Jesus, a miracle had to be performed. So, on the third day, after Jesus died on the cross, He was resurrected, demonstrating the omnipotence of God.

This very act was the act that would cause people to believe in a god that reigns supreme and holds the power of the universe in His very hands, a god that could save them from themselves.

Today, if you are an unbeliever, you can change your destiny. You can change where you will spend your eternity. Our Heavenly Father gives us the freedom of choice about how we want to live our life here on earth and how we want to spend eternity. In Deuteronomy 30:19, God boldly declares, *"I call heaven and earth to record this day against you, that I have set before you life and death, blessing and cursing: therefore choose life, that both thou and thy seed may live."*

So, dear friend what choice will you make today? Will you spend your eternity with the Creator or will you suffer Hell's eternal flames? Again, the choice is yours. Just as the men aboard the ship who were with Jonah became believers, you too can make a choice to accept the only one and true living God as your god.

If after reading the above passages, you have decided that you want to spend your eternity in Heaven with God, the Creator, and His son Jesus, and the Holy Spirit, read through what has affectionately come to be known as the Roman's Road. This is the road to salvation. As you read through the scriptures that comprise the Roman's Road, you will also read the explanation for each scripture, so you will have clarity about what you are reading and confessing.

The Roman's Road to Salvation

The road to salvation begins with Romans 3:23 which declares, "*For all have sinned, and come short of the glory of God.*" This scripture explains that everyone has come short of God's glory and needs redemption. Then, Romans 6:23a states, "*For the wages of sin is death.*" Here, we learn that the consequence of living a life of sin is death. Everyone will experience physical death as a result of the sin committed in the garden of Eden, but those who commit themselves to a life of sin will suffer eternal damnation in the lake of fire (Rev. 19). Continue with the rest of verse 6:23 that says, "*but the gift of God is eternal life through Jesus Christ our Lord.*" There is an alternative to suffering eternal damnation. We can accept the gift of salvation by accepting Jesus as our personal Lord and Savior. Then, Romans 5:8 says, "*But God commendeth his love toward us, in that, while we were yet sinners, Christ died for us.*" We are able to receive the gift of salvation because Christ came to earth and shed His blood for us on the cross.

Continue to Romans 10: 9-10 which says, "*That if thou shalt confess with thy mouth the Lord Jesus, and shalt believe in thine heart that God hath raised him from the dead, thou shalt be saved. For with the heart man believeth unto righteousness; and with the mouth confession is made unto salvation.*" If we confess with our mouths that Jesus is the son of God, that He came and died for our sins, and that God raised Him from the dead, we will receive salvation.

Finish with Romans 10:13, which states, *"For whosoever shall call upon the name of the Lord shall be saved."* Call upon the name of God by saying these words, **"Lord Jesus, come into my heart and save me, Lord. I believe that you are the Son of God who came and died on the cross for my sins. I believe that you rose from the grave. I also believe that you now sit in heaven on the right side of the Father, making intercession for me. I accept you as my Lord and my Savior."**

Now that you have confessed with your mouth that Jesus is the son of God and that He died for our sins and rose from the grave, **YOU ARE NOW SAVED!!!!** You will spend your eternity in heaven.

The next step is very important- you must find a Bible-based church that teaches the Word of God and confesses the Lord Jesus Christ to be the son of God. Don't delay. Do this immediately. Do not leave yourself open to the enemy. Get connected with the saints of the Most High God and keep yourself covered with the unspotted blood of the Lamb.

Here is my prayer for you.
Father God,

I thank you for the opportunity to minister your word to the unsaved, the unchurched, and the uncommitted. Father God, I pray now for the souls who have just received the gift of salvation. Lord Father, they have opened their hearts to you, and I know that you have received them into your kingdom and written their names in the Book of Life. Father God, I pray that you will touch their lives and show yourself mightily before them. Let their eyes be opened by the scales falling off, allowing them to see clearly.

Father God, I even pray for the backslider, those who have turned away from you after receiving the gift of salvation. You said in your Word that you desire that none would perish. So Lord, I send your Word to them right now, praying that they would confess the iniquity in their heart, repent, and turn from their evil ways, so that they may receive a life of abundance. You said in your Word in Matthew Chapter 14, that every knee shall bow before you and every tongue will confess that Jesus is Lord.

Father God, I pray now that we all come under subjection to your Word and that we will humbly submit our lives to you. I ask all these things in the name of my Lord and Savior Jesus Christ.

Amen, Amen, Amen!!!!

I will continue to pray for your success in your walk with God. Remember, this spiritual walk that you are about to embark on will not be an easy walk, but remember, the race is not given to the swift but to those who endure to the end.

Be blessed with heaven's best. I love you!

About the Author

Dr. Cassundra White-Elliott is a dynamic and multi-faceted individual, excelling in various roles as an educator, English professor, author, publisher, and minister. With a strong foundation in education, literature, and faith-based leadership, Dr. White-Elliott has dedicated her career to fostering growth, empowerment, spiritual awareness, and social change.

Starting her academic journey with a Bachelor of Arts in Education, Dr. White-Elliott laid the groundwork for her passion for teaching and learning. She recognized the power of education as a tool for transformation and dedicated herself to empowering students to reach their full potential.

Building upon her undergraduate studies, Dr. White-Elliott pursued a Master of Arts in English Composition, delving deep into the intricacies of writer's agency and voice. Armed with a keen under-standing of the written word, she honed her skills as a writer, educator, and advocate for marginalized voices in literature.

Continuing her quest for knowledge and expertise, Dr. White-Elliott earned her Ph.D. in Education, specializing in curriculum development and professional studies. Her doctoral research focused on African American English Vernacular and educational biases against its use.

As an educator, Dr. White-Elliott brings passion, creativity, and expertise to her role as an English professor. Through engaging lectures, thought-provoking discussions, and innovative teaching methods, she inspires students to explore the complexities of literature, language, and culture while fostering critical thinking and empathy.

Outside of academia, Dr. White-Elliott is a prolific author, using her writing to amplify marginalized voices and advocate for social change. Her published works span a wide range of genres, from scholarly articles and essays to faith-based and fictional novels, exploring themes of spirituality and social justice.

Driven by a desire to provide a platform for underrepresented writers, Dr. White-Elliott founded a publishing company (CLF Publishing Collaborative, LLC), dedicated to promoting diverse voices and empowering authors to share their stories with the world. As the founder and CEO, she strives to challenge stereotypes, dismantle barriers, and foster understanding and empathy across diverse communities.

In addition to her academic and literary pursuits, Dr. White-Elliott is also a dedicated minister, guiding individuals on their spiritual journeys and fostering a sense of community and belonging. With a focus on love, compassion, and individual growth, she uses her platform as a minister to advocate for the Body of Christ to operate in the spirit of unity while fulfilling their God-given callings.

Overall, Dr. Cassundra White-Elliott's journey is a testament to the power of education, writing, and faith in driving positive change in the world. Through her dedication, passion, and unwavering commitment to changing lives, she continues to inspire others to embrace learning, celebrate diversity, and work towards a more just and equitable society.

Additional Titles by the Author

Pub. Speaking in the Spiritual Arena (2002)
Do You Know God? (2004)
Unleashed Anger, Anger Unleashed (2005)
Unleashed Anger Daily Prayer (2005)
Two of a Kind (2006)
Dare to Succeed by Breaking Through Barriers (2007)
Dare to Succeed Prayer Guide (2007)
Through the Storm (2007)
Lord, Teach Me to be a Blessing! (2007)
The Preacher's Daughter (2007)
The Preacher's Son (2009)
Where is Your Joppa? (2009)
From Despair, through Determination, to Victory! (2009)
Fear Not (2011)
Mayhem in the Hamptons (2012)
After the Dust Settles (2013)
A Mother's Heart (2013)
A Diamond in the Rough (2013)
The Power of a Woman (2013)
365 Days of Encouragement (2013)
A Touch in the Dark (2014)
Broken Chains (2014)
I Have Fallen (2014)
The Bottom Line (2015)
Set Free (2015)
Daughter, God Loves You (2016)
A Mother's Heart II (2016)
Living a Balanced Life (2016)
Kimara & Aaron…Disneyland (2016)
Embracing Womanhood (2017)
A Mother's Heart III (2017)
Web of Lies (2017)
Time is Running Out (2017)

Revisiting Grammar & Business Writing Essentials (2017)
Test Preparation: Writing Essentials, Mathematics Review & Reasoning Skills (2017)
The Making of Dr. C. (2018)
Claim Your Inheritance (2018)
Women's Study Bible New International Version (2018)
Christian Inspiration (2019-present)
Safety in Him (2019)
A Mother's Heart IV (2019)
A is for Adam (2019)
Have You Walked in My Shoes? (2019)
Prepare for Battle (2019)
Christian Inspiration Magazine (2019-2023)
B is for Babel (2020)
C is for Christ (2020)
D is for David (2020)
E is Eve (2020)
F is for Forgiveness (2020)
G is for Givers (2020)
H is for Helping Others (2020)
I is for Idols (2020)
J is for Joseph (2020)
K is for Kindness (2020)
The Last Shall Be First: An Analysis of the Systemic Subdivide of Black America (2021)
L is for Love (2021)
M is for Mary (2021)
N is for Noah's Ark (2021)
O is for Obedience (2021)
Rest in Him: Scriptures for Daily Peace (2021)
P is for Paul the Apostle (2021)
Q is for Queen Esther (2021)
Be Ye Inspired Vol. 1 (2021)

R is for Ruth (2021)
Be Ye Inspired Vol. II (2022)
S is for Samuel (2022)
T is for Truth (2022)
U is for Unconditional Love (2022)
V is for Victory (2022)
W is for Worship (2022)
X is for Xerxes (2022)
Y is for You (2022)
Pearls of Wisdom (2022)
Z is for Zachariah (2022)
Be Ye Inspired Vol II (2022)
Pearls of Wisdom Quotes & Journal (2022)
Shift Your Narrative (2023)
Without a Mask (2023)
Naked Before God (2024)
Dismantling Systemic Racism and Its Effects (2024)
Be Ye Inspired Vol III (2024)

www.ingramcontent.com/pod-product-compliance
Lightning Source LLC
Chambersburg PA
CBHW071403160426
42813CB00083B/437